Coco The Cat

(A bedtime story)

By Andrew Taylor

ISBN: 978-1-917293-83-9

This book is dedicated with love,
to Darcie my granddaughter,
and to Tricia, her grandmother.

Coco The Cat Visits

Coco was a black cat with shiny black
fur, a white nose, and green eyes.
He lived next door.
He came to say hello every morning.
He used the cat flap!
He always made us smile.
He always said ...

Meeow!

Coco Comes To Stay

Coco loved to be with us,
but didn't like to be touched.
He was good at catching mice.
Dad said he was feral.
Which means he was wild!
Like a tiger....grrrr!

The family next door moved away
and gave Dad the cat.
'He spends most of his time
at yours anyway.'
So Coco became our cat.

Meeow!

The School Bag

Early one morning, Dad was making
tea and talking to Coco.
He did this every morning.
Coco didn't talk back, but Dad
talked to him anyway.

When I came down, Coco was
sitting on my school bag.
I picked it up and Coco jumped off.
The bag was heavy with
all the books for the day.

Coco followed me to the car
and watched me leave.

My teacher told me to get my books
out, but when I opened my bag,
I saw a mouse!
I told the teacher,
'Miss, I have a mouse in my bag!'

She didn't believe me.
She put her hand in my bag to get
my book and the mouse bit her!
Then it jumped out of my bag
and made its escape.
It ran around the room and the
children screamed and climbed up
onto their desks.

Miss went for the caretaker.
The caretaker opened all the doors
and the mouse ran outside
to freedom.

Coco caught lots of mice.
Dad said he was a good mouser.
He often brought mice home
as a gift for Mum and Dad.
As a kind of thank you.

He must have accidentally dropped
the mouse in my school bag.

Meeow!

Dad Got A New Job

We moved house to a new town
and a new school.
We had to buy a cat carrier.
Coco didn't like the journey!
When we got there, we put butter
on Coco's paws.
Dad said it was so he could find
his way home.

Yumm yumm!

Our new house was very modern.
Lots of glass windows and
glass doors, but no cat flap.

So, Coco would throw himself
at the window to tell us he wanted
to come in!

He did this ...
if it was raining,
if he was hungry,
or if he wanted to watch TV...
(he especially liked
wildlife documentaries).

Mum asked Dad,
'Andy, can you put a cat flap
on the garden shed?'
So Coco got his own home.

Meeow!

The Vet

There was a fast road outside the
school that was very dangerous.

Coco went mousing
and got hit by a car!
He crawled back home.
He must have been in a lot of pain,
but he knew where home was
because of the butter.

Meeow ow ow ow!

Dad rang the vet.
The vet took Coco away.
He said he could put Coco to sleep,
or he could rebuild his leg,
which would be expensive.
Mum told Dad,
'Andy, use the Venice money.'

The surgeon operated on Coco,
using pins and screws to rebuild
his leg. Coco had to stay in a big cage
in the front room for six weeks.
Coco was very angry.
But Dad said he was now a bionic cat!

Meeeeeeyeow!

Time To Say Goodnight...

Coco lived a long and happy life.
He was never a pet,
more a companion.

Dad said, 'Coco was talismanic in the
changing good fortunes of our family.'

I think that means, he brought us
good luck! When Coco arrived,
everything went well for everyone.

Mum said he went to look after some other children.

We always smile when we think of Coco the Cat.

And now, so will you.

Whisper...

Meeeow xxx

About the Author

Andrew Taylor has enjoyed a life in education spanning 35 years: as Headmaster, Housemaster, and Head of History. The last 22 years of his career were spent at the Benedictine schools of Douai and Worth, where both of his sons were educated. In retirement, he sits on the committee of The Worth Society and he is a Trustee of The Douai Foundation.